RIVER

through the

DESERT

Advance Praise for
River through the Desert

"This Lenten resources holds the possibility of transforming our difficult experiences of the last few years by offering the possibility of seeing them as a gift, a place of refreshment and hope."

—The Rt. Revd. Sarah Mullally
Bishop of London

RIVER
through the
DESERT

*a lenten journey
in the holy land*

Richard Sewell

St. George's College
Jerusalem • 2022

St. George's College
P.O. Box 1248
33 Salah El Deen Street
Jerusalem 91000
www.saintgeorgescollegejerusalem.com

ISBN: 979-8-405-10755-4

CONTENTS

FOREWORD

The Rev. Dr. Susan Lukens

Associate Dean Emerita
St. George's College, Jerusalem

During my years at St. George's College, I was privileged to share many grace-filled moments with pilgrims seeking God in the holy places of Jerusalem, Ein Karem, Nazareth, and the environs of Palestine. It was clear when Dean Richard arrived in the fall of 2018 that his gentle ways would enhance the spirit of pilgrimage at St. George's College; he would help us search for God in what the Celts call "thin places." Working together remotely and in person, I have found that Richard's gifts helped me in my own quest to understand what it means to be God's disciple called to love and serve.

In the winter of 2020, when COVID restrictions had seriously complicated the possibility of pilgrimage, Dean Richard made a series of meditations available electronically so that people could continue to journey through the Holy Land in spirit. After I first read through these reflections and watched the videos, I thought that Richard's words would make an inspirational Lenten book. As I delved further into the reflections and videos, I knew publishing a book should be the next step. Our conversation began in earnest.

i

You have in your hand the start of a Lenten journey in the Land of the Holy One. You will soon discover that Richard invites you each week to a sacred space. You will find yourself immersed in the landscape as you journey in the desert for answers, climb high up a mountain to be nearer to God, rest on the shore of the Galilee in order to find "the call of Christ in your life," and walk with Richard along the ancient roads until you finally enter a garden paradise. In all of these places, he reflects on the Biblical history and spirituality of this holy place.

At this juncture in our history, when travel is problematic, this Lenten pilgrimage gives us a chance to be pilgrims, traveling to the Holy Land and imagining the gifts unveiled by landscapes that become integral to our understanding of the Lenten season and our own thirst for God.

This Lenten season gives us permission to find a time for sabbath rest, to be in silence and in prayer. It allows a time for imagining ourselves in the land of the Holy One where Jesus' life, death and resurrection took place. May you place your joys, sorrows, and woes at the foot of the cross, and in doing so, may you find the grace of spiritual love, forgiveness, and renewal in this Lenten journey. My hope is that you will find, as I have, a spiritual guide in *River through the Desert*.

Seeking God's Grace,
Susan

INTRODUCTION

This Lenten resource offers a taste of the beauty, wonder, and inspiration of the Holy Land. For people who have been to the Holy Land it will be a reminder of those times which undoubtedly have left an indelible impression. For people who have not yet made their pilgrimage, it can serve as a taster to inspire a visit to the Land of the Holy One. For any who will not be able to travel to Israel and Palestine, it can serve as an alternative way of experiencing the spiritual riches of these lands.

The coronavirus pandemic caused the closure of St. George's College in early March 2020. It remained closed for two years with no pilgrims able to stay in the College. The closure inspired me to consider how to engage with people during an enforced fallow period. This Lenten study is unusual because alongside this written material, there are six short films which are an important part of each week's resources. Links to the films are provided in the study. The films bring something of the wonders of the Holy Land, the cradle of the Abrahamic faiths, to you wherever you are.

The Holy Land has been called (probably first by Eusebius of Caesarea) the 'Fifth Gospel.' The reason for this name is that, just as the written Gospels testify to the word and works of Jesus Christ, so the land itself conveys that same message, with the eyes of faith. We talk about 'salvation history' as the Christian narrative from Abraham and Sarah through to Jesus, as the way that hope unfolded for humanity. We can also talk about the Holy Land as communicating the 'geography of salvation' because the land has the potential to convey the gospel of Jesus Christ in a very powerful way. This at least is the testimony of many millions of pilgrims who come to Israel and Palestine every year.

I have written this study course drawing on the ways in which the land here has touched and deepened my faith over my time living in Jerusalem and serving as the Dean of the College. I have also drawn on experiences in my home country, Great Britain, which have enriched my faith. My hope is that the reader will be drawn to think about the ways in which their own context and its geography can draw them into a deeper relationship with God this Lent.

This Lenten series is called *River through the Desert* because a Lenten course should seek to water faith in the same way that a river causes the desert to flower and flourish in unexpected ways. In the trying and testing days of the pandemic we stood in need, perhaps more than ever, of finding solace and encouragement in faith to give strength to endure these challenges. God's grace is always sufficient to endure whatever difficulties are faced. It is my hope that this course can be a vehicle for God's grace.

Blessings of the Holy One from the Holy City,
Richard Sewell
Dean of St George's College, Jerusalem
Epiphanytide 2022

I am about to do a new thing;
    now it springs forth,
    do you not perceive it?
I will make a way in the wilderness
    and rivers in the desert.

ISAIAH 43:19

WEEK ONE
THE
DESERT

The desert blooming in spring

1. *Reflection*

The desert has profound significance in the Christian life. We are most readily drawn to think about the desert because of Jesus's temptations there which mark the beginning of his public ministry. But that significant moment evokes the much earlier foundational event of the Exodus of the Hebrew people who escaped the clutches of Pharaoh on a long journey towards the 'Promised Land.'

Those forty years wandering in the desert before crossing the Jordan into a new homeland create a framework for understanding Jesus's own Moses-like role as a liberator of enslaved peoples. In his role as God's Messiah, he is to be the Saviour of all humanity.

The Hebrews wandered for forty years and Jesus endured forty days of temptation in the Judean desert before he was fully ready to serve God in his role as Messiah. Historically, the desert took on great significance for the church because of the establishment of monasteries in the wildernesses of Egypt and Palestine from the fourth century. These in turn inspired the rather different monastic movements of the medieval European church. This has left an indelible imprint on Christian life in our own times in the form of a pattern of regular daily prayer and of the study of scriptures, both of which were and still are essential to monastic life. It is part of the purpose of the season of Lent to renew our life of prayer and thoughtful consideration of our discipleship as Christians.

Inevitably the desert can be a somewhat unappealing idea to us if we have little knowledge or experience of desert wildernesses. For Jesus, then, and for those who live in the Holy Land today, the desert is just a normal feature of the landscape. I grew up living on the edge of a huge area of moorland in England. I loved to explore the moors then and still do when I return home now. However, I was taught to respect the moor and not to underestimate its dangers. It is the same with the desert which is just ten miles from where I live now at St George's College in Jerusalem.

"Then Jesus was led up by the Spirit into the wilderness to be tempted by the devil. He fasted for forty days and forty nights and afterwards he was famished" (Matt 4:1-2).

The Gospels tell us that, when Jesus was baptized, he received the divine affirmation—"You are my Son, the Beloved" (Mark 1:11)—and he was then

The Judean Desert

drawn into an effort of endurance and temptation. Tradition has it that this occurred in the Judean desert between Jerusalem and the River Jordan. It is inhospitable, the climate is hot, and there would have been wild and dangerous animals. But if you imagine this desert as endless miles of Saharan sand dunes, then you have the wrong image.

The picture above shows that this desert is rocky terrain, not sandy, and there are hills and ravines. Throughout this desert there are streams in the summer and rivers in the winter. There is shade, shelter, and refreshment. Although the ground is arid and rocky, surprisingly, in the spring, grasses and flowers grow up as can be seen in the first photo above. Despite this being desert, vegetation does grow, so Jesus would not have been without the means to stave off death by thirst or starvation if he had chosen to do so. But, vitally, this desert is a place of isolation, away from the distractions of people and the normal demands of everyday life. It is an opportunity to escape and contemplate the essence and purpose of life. The desert wilderness gave to Jesus then, as it gives to people now, the chance to strip away our preoccupations and to focus on the presence of God. It is an awe-inspiring landscape that draws our attention towards the eternal and the profound.

Part of the opportunity of Lent is to willingly allow ourselves to be taken into a metaphorical desert. It might seem to be a bleak prospect, but when we know the reality of the desert, we need not be fearful of it. It is a way to detach ourselves from some of the trappings of our life which feel indispensable but actually, we might find ourselves liberated to be without them.

There are also unexpected pleasures in the desert such as flowers, fruit, water, and shade. All are more precious because we might not have anticipated them. Likewise, time in a 'spiritual desert' should not simply be about what we do without, but rather what we might surprisingly find. The opportunity in Lent to find some 'desert time' is not simply about a time of deprivation; we can see it as a time of enrichment.

Jesus confronted the devil and resisted the temptations in his desert time, but I like to imagine that it gave to him far more than just that. He

A river flows in Wadi Qelt in spring

discovered the strength to equip himself for the demands which lay ahead. He benefitted from time
away from the ordinary demands of everyday life. It
allowed him to think deeply about his calling, which
had just been made plain to him at the Jordan River.
Likewise, the Hebrews wandered for forty years,
seemingly without purpose. However, they learned

7

St. George Choziba Monastery in Wadi Qelt

some vital lessons about how to serve and worship Yahweh and about their life in community whilst they were there. Perhaps without that time in the desert, their arrival in the Promised Land would have been less fruitful.

In the Judean desert one can also be surprised to find a monastery nestled into a valley or hidden in the midst of an oasis. Monks still live here in these isolated communities. They commit themselves to a life in the desert not as a punishment, but as a gift. These monasteries are not simply archaic remnants of a former time, they stand as a physical reminder to us that we are all called to a life of prayer and contemplation.

Alan Jones, sometime Dean of Grace Cathedral, San Francisco, wrote a wonderful book entitled *Soul Making: The Desert Way of Spirituality*. In it he wrote,

"The desert is a place of the encounter with death. It is also the place where we know ourselves to be truly free. We do not go into the desert to wall up our heart. We go there in order to give it away to God and to the world."

Most people cannot find a desert to spend time in during Lent but there are other types of wildernesses which may be accessible. Perhaps you could find a metaphorical desert of the heart. These might prove to be fruitful places to spend time contemplating the presence of God and God's all redeeming love. May it be a place where you find a new sense of freedom.

2. *Watch the Film*

The film for Week 1, "The Desert," can be accessed by typing https://youtu.be/bI99-Sj7_jY into your browser. Alternatively, use the QR code on your mobile or cell phone.

3. *Read the Scriptures*

This week, reflect on the Gospel of Matthew 4:1-11. Read the passage once or twice and spend some time considering the details of the story.

¹ Then Jesus was led up by the Spirit into the wilderness to be tempted by the devil. ² He fasted forty days and forty nights, and afterwards he was famished. ³ The tempter came and said to him, "If you are the Son of God, command these stones to become loaves of bread." ⁴ But he answered, "It is written,

> 'One does not live by bread alone,
>> but by every word that comes from
>>> the mouth of God.'"

⁵ Then the devil took him to the holy city and placed him on the pinnacle of the temple, ⁶ saying to him, "If you are the Son of God, throw yourself down; for it is written,

> 'He will command his angels concerning you,'
>> and 'On their hands they will bear you up,
> so that you will not dash your foot against a
>> stone.'"

⁷ Jesus said to him, "Again it is written, 'Do not put the Lord your God to the test.'"

⁸ Again, the devil took him to a very high mountain and showed him all the kingdoms of the world and their splendor; ⁹ and he said to him, "All these I will give you, if you will fall down and worship me." ¹⁰ Jesus said to him, "Away with you, Satan! for it is written,

> 'Worship the Lord your God,
>> and serve only him.'"

¹¹ Then the devil left him, and suddenly angels came and waited on him.

4. *Ask Questions*

1. Does the idea of time in some kind of wilderness draw you or concern you? Why?

2. Is there an accessible place which could serve as a 'desert' to you? What do you, or could you, gain from spending time there?

3. In what ways might Jesus have been changed or strengthened by his testing in the desert? Could this be true for you and if so, how?

4. Is there a word or phrase that resonates for you in the quote from Alan Jones' *Soul Making*? As you ponder this, is there an invitation from God for you?

5. The reflection above mentions the surprises which can be found in the desert. Have you ever been surprised by time in solitude or in an isolated place?

6. You might like to do a drawing, write a poem or express yourself creatively in some other way to represent what the desert means to you.

You might like to spend some time in prayer.

You might like to reflect further on this session and write down anything you want to hold on to.

WEEK TWO

THE
WELL

A spring at Ein Gedi in the desert

1. *Reflection*

Water is a vital element in the sustenance of human life. We can survive without water to drink for four days, at most. In ancient civilisations, dwellings would only be built around, or near, a reliable fresh water supply. In Jerusalem, it was the Gihon Spring in the Kidron Valley which enabled King David to make the city his capital. If there was no spring, then an underwater supply would need to be found and a well could be built over it to enable water to be collected and carried.

In ancient Israel—as across the entire hot and dry climate of the Middle East where water is not readily available—springs, wells, and cisterns were especially important because there was not enough rainwater to sustain life for humans or animals. This Lent course, entitled *River through the Desert*, is itself a reminder of the significance of water to the essence of life. For those of us who have not grown up in such a climate or culture, there is much to learn about living in a society where water is such a

Bronze Age remains of Shechem in the midst of modern Nablus

precious commodity. It is challenging for us that sci-
entists predict that the climate crisis is going to
make water shortages—and conflicts arising from
this—a far more common part of life around the
world.

In the light of all this, it is not surprising that
water in its many forms features significantly in the
Bible, in both Old and New Testaments. Once again
there are resonances between the two halves of our
Scripture which provide a rich vein of study for us.
Perhaps this is never more true than in the story of
the Samaritan woman at the well (John 4:1-42), a
story unique to the fourth gospel. Right at the start
of the narrative, allusion is made to former times by
reference to 'the Samaritan town of Sychar, near the
plot of ground that Jacob had given to his son, Joseph' and to Jacob's well there (John 4:5-6).

Sychar also goes by the name Shechem and is
now a significant town in the West Bank, called Nablus. Abram and Sarai pass through Shechem (Gen
12:4-9), but it is their grandson, Jacob, who settles

16

there with his family. Thereafter, in the Bible, it becomes an important Jewish town.

It is another water well, many miles away, where Jacob first meets Rachel, falls in love with her and later marries her (Gen 29:1-12). They meet at the well because Jacob needs a drink and Rachel brings her flock of sheep to the same place for them to be refreshed. This story beautifully illustrates the significant role that wells served, fulfilling the practical and vital purpose of satisfying thirst and also serving as a place of meeting. It was the duty of young women to make the daily journeys to the well to get the households' water supply. Because of this, men knew that if they wished to 'chance upon' a particular young woman, this was a good place to do so. In addition to Jacob, Abraham and Moses also found their wives in just such a way.

All of this is important context for the remarkable and highly instructive story of Jesus's encounter with a Samaritan woman at Jacob's well in Shechem. This one story, recounted beautifully in John's Gospel, has so much within it that I cannot possibly do full justice to it in this short study. We will just deal with a few points to help us to begin sounding its depths.

As with all Jesus's dealings with Samaritans in the Gospels, this is a boundary and prejudice challenging message. Samaritans were the remnant of the northern kingdom of Israel. This nation was defeated in the eighth century BC, and the people scattered. Thereafter, Samaritans were treated with

Icon in the Church of St. Photina, Nablus

scorn and contempt by the southern kingdom of Judah ('the Jews'). Interestingly, the Samaritan people and religion remains to this day. The community is centered in Nablus, and their worship takes place on Mount Gerazim, in that vicinity. By engaging with Samaritans, Jesus was breaking taboos and undermining the prejudice of the Jews who treated

*Jacob's Well in the crypt chapel
of the Church of St. Photina, Nablus*

Samaritans as heretics and tried to avoid mixing with them altogether.

The church built over the well in ancient Shechem—modern-day Nablus—is fascinating. It is not on every pilgrim groups' itinerary, but it never fails to move all the groups that we ever take there. Under the watchful and paternalistic eye of the Greek Orthodox priest of the Church of St. Photina the Samaritan Woman, the building has become a rich tapestry of beautiful icons all over the church. The ancient well itself, situated in the crypt and no longer in the open air, still evokes something of the encounter between Christ and the Samaritan woman. The icons surrounding it draw our close attention to their fascinating dialogue.

Mary's Well at Ein Kerem

The text tells us that the encounter took place at noon (John 4:6). This is not the usual time of day to come to draw water unless you are wanting to avoid meeting people.

Jesus is sitting by the well when the woman arrives, and rather than stepping away as convention required to indicate no bad intentions, Jesus asks her to draw water for him. She is shocked because for a Jew to speak to a Samaritan and for a man to speak to an unaccompanied woman was very much not the norm. This, of course, is the other boundary which we see Jesus transgressing. The significance of this may not have been fully comprehended for many generations, but this story has become an inspiration for the liberation of women in the church and in wider society in modern times. It is hard to overstress how challenging to cultural norms Jesus's engagement with the Samaritan woman was.

It is a deep tragedy that, despite such prejudice-defying accounts of Jesus's life and teaching, the Church and the contexts in which it is situated throughout the world continue to perpetuate racism and sexism, which damages all of us. It is also important to remember that Christians (and all Palestinians) are on the receiving end of dreadful racism at the hands of those Jewish Israelis who do not acknowledge the right of Palestinians to live in their historic lands. Incidents of harassment and violence occur today in Nablus by Jewish settlers against Palestinians living there. Clearly, anti-Semitism is also a continuing cancer in the world today.

The Samaritan woman is an inspiring example of an assertive and articulate woman who Jesus affirms and further empowers. According to fifth-century Greek tradition, she is called St. Photina (meaning 'enlightened' or 'luminous') because she became convinced that Jesus was the promised Messiah and she testified about him in the city and 'many Samaritans from that city believed in him because of her testimony' (John 4:39). Perhaps she should be acknowledged as the first female Christian preacher and an example for all people.

Here in this place, in the hot and dusty climate of the Holy Land, beside an ancient water well, we are reminded that Jesus is the living water who can satisfy our deepest thirst for meaning and purpose in life. We are challenged to do as St. Photina did: to proclaim that Jesus is 'truly the Saviour of the world' (John 4:42) and that he breaks down walls of division.

2. *Watch the Film*

 The film for Week 2, "The Well," can be accessed by typing https://youtu.be/7p3qlBwTuNY into your browser. Alternatively, use the QR code on your mobile or cell phone.

3. *Read the Scriptures*

This week, reflect on the Gospel of John 4:1-42. Read the passage once or twice and spend some time considering the details of the story.

1 Now when Jesus learned that the Pharisees had heard, "Jesus is making and baptizing more disciples than John" 2 —although it was not Jesus himself but his disciples who baptized— 3 he left Judea and started back to Galilee. 4 But he had to go through Samaria. 5 So he came to a Samaritan city called Sychar, near the plot of ground that Jacob had given to his son Joseph. 6 Jacob's well was there, and Jesus, tired out by his journey, was sitting by the well. It was about noon.

7 A Samaritan woman came to draw water, and Jesus said to her, "Give me a drink." 8 (His disciples had gone to the city to buy food.) 9 The Samaritan woman said to him, "How is it that you, a Jew, ask a drink of me, a woman of Samaria?" (Jews do not share things in common with Samaritans.) 10 Jesus answered her, "If you knew the gift of God, and who it is that is saying to you, 'Give me a drink,' you would have asked him, and he would have given you living water." 11 The woman said to him, "Sir, you have no bucket, and the well is deep. Where do you get that living water? 12 Are you greater than our ancestor Jacob, who gave us the well, and with his sons and his flocks drank from it?" 13 Jesus said to her, "Everyone who drinks of this water will be thirsty again, 14 but those who drink of the water that I will give them will never be thirsty. The water that I will give will become in them a spring of water gushing up to eternal life." 15 The woman said to him, "Sir, give me this water, so that I may never be thirsty or have to keep coming here to draw water."

16 Jesus said to her, "Go, call your husband, and come back." 17 The woman answered him, "I have no husband." Jesus said to her, "You are right in saying, 'I have no husband'; 18 for you have had five husbands, and the one you have now is not your husband. What you have said is true!" 19 The woman said to him, "Sir, I see that you are a prophet. 20 Our ancestors worshiped on this mountain, but you say that the place where people must worship is in Jerusalem." 21 Jesus said to her, "Woman, believe me, the

hour is coming when you will worship the Father neither on this mountain nor in Jerusalem. ²² You worship what you do not know; we worship what we know, for salvation is from the Jews. ²³ But the hour is coming, and is now here, when the true worshipers will worship the Father in spirit and truth, for the Father seeks such as these to worship him. ²⁴ God is spirit, and those who worship him must worship in spirit and truth." ²⁵ The woman said to him, "I know that Messiah is coming" (who is called Christ). "When he comes, he will proclaim all things to us." ²⁶ Jesus said to her, "I am he, the one who is speaking to you."

²⁷ Just then his disciples came. They were astonished that he was speaking with a woman, but no one said, "What do you want?" or, "Why are you speaking with her?" ²⁸ Then the woman left her water jar and went back to the city. She said to the people, ²⁹ "Come and see a man who told me everything I have ever done! He cannot be the Messiah, can he?" ³⁰ They left the city and were on their way to him.

³¹ Meanwhile the disciples were urging him, "Rabbi, eat something." ³² But he said to them, "I have food to eat that you do not know about." ³³ So the disciples said to one another, "Surely no one has brought him something to eat?" ³⁴ Jesus said to them, "My food is to do the will of him who sent me and to complete his work. ³⁵ Do you not say, 'Four months more, then comes the harvest'? But I tell you, look around you, and see how the fields are ripe

24

for harvesting. [36] The reaper is already receiving wages and is gathering fruit for eternal life, so that sower and reaper may rejoice together. [37] For here the saying holds true, 'One sows and another reaps.' [38] I sent you to reap that for which you did not labor. Others have labored, and you have entered into their labor."

[39] Many Samaritans from that city believed in him because of the woman's testimony, "He told me everything I have ever done." [40] So when the Samaritans came to him, they asked him to stay with them; and he stayed there two days. [41] And many more believed because of his word. [42] They said to the woman, "It is no longer because of what you said that we believe, for we have heard for ourselves, and we know that this is truly the Savior of the world."

4. Ask Questions

1. John's description of Jesus's conversation with the Samaritan woman makes a play on physical thirst and spiritual thirst. What is your experience of spiritual thirst? How is that thirst quenched for you?

2. Spend some time looking at the icon. In icons there is a deep significance in hand gestures, head position, and eyes. Consider what is said in the film. What do you see? What might it mean? The rock formations represent Mount Gerazim and Mount Ebal which surround Shechem

(modern-day Nablus). What else do you see in the icon?

3. Jesus's teaching powerfully challenges prejudices relating to ethnicity (Gentiles and Samaritans) and to gender. Have you experienced such prejudice in the church directed at yourself, or others? What has been your response to this? What other lessons can be taken from this story?

4. Spend some time reflecting on how the woman's feelings would have changed through the complexities of this encounter with Jesus. Reflect on this in the light of the Eucharist. How are we made hungry and thirsty and how are these needs satisfied? What are you thirsty for?

You might like to spend some time in prayer.

You might like to reflect further on this session and write down anything you want to hold on to.

WEEK THREE

THE
MOUNTAIN

Mount Tabor in Galilee

1. *Reflection*

A thoughtful reading of the Bible shows that many of the themes and important events in the New Testament are prefigured by themes and events in the Old Testament. This will hold true for much of what we consider in this Lent course. As mentioned before, Matthew, in his gospel account, can be seen to be presenting Jesus as a new Moses leading people out of slavery into liberation. So, it is not surprising that the mountain of Sinai should find some reflections in the life of Jesus.

Throughout the Old Testament, significant events occur in high places: Elijah's showdown with the prophets of Baal, the giving of the Ten Commandments on Sinai, and King David choosing a 'mountain' (Mount Zion) in Jerusalem to place the Ark of the Covenant. That site is identified with the same mountain where Abraham proved willing to take the life of his son, Isaac, as an offering to God. It is also the same place that King Solomon constructed the Jerusalem Temple. Indeed, Jerusalem,

The Mount of Olives in Jerusalem

the Holy City, is a city 'built on my holy hill' (Ps 2:6). Jerusalem covers several hills often called 'mountains' or 'mounts', for example, the Mount of Olives which is so familiar to Christians. In reality, 'hill' feels like a more accurate description on the basis of its height.

It should not surprise us at all that significant events take place on mountains in Jesus's life too. All of this is not accidental. Early Jewish thinking structured creation in three tiers with a literal understanding of the heavens above the earth and the underworld beneath the earth. In their thinking, God did literally live in the heavens. As a result, the top of a mountain brought one nearer to the presence of God and encounters with God could be expected to occur on those high places. Once again,

30

the treasured account of Jesus's Sermon on the Mount (Matt 5:1-12), when he gave to the people a framework for living, is suggestive of Moses who came down Mount Sinai with the Ten Commandments. Moses had to go up the mountain for his encounter with the Lord; he needed to be high up and, therefore, near to God.

In our own times we might wistfully look to the sky seeking a word from God to guide or comfort us, but we do not seriously imagine 'up there' as the actual dwelling place of God. We surely know that God cannot be confined by space or time. And yet we might still have a sense that a walk up a high hill or a mountain could be an opportunity for a profound spiritual experience. It is often said that such locations are 'thin places' where the space between heaven and earth seems particularly permeable. In such places, we might feel the presence of God in an especially powerful way.

On occasion, Jesus seems to have encouraged the same thing with his disciples. Soon after Peter's declaration to Jesus that 'you are the Messiah, the Son of the living God' (Matt 16:16), Jesus takes a few of his closest disciples 'up a high mountain.' Since the 4th century AD, this has been identified as Mount Tabor a few miles to the west of the Sea of Galilee. It rises sharply up from the Valley of Jezreel and dominates the landscape. Up on the mountain, Jesus is transfigured by a bright shining light and the disciples have a profound religious experience—the prophets Moses and Elijah appear amongst them.

The Jezreel Valley from the top of Mount Tabor

This might seem strange to us, but the disciples, though shocked, would have made the necessary connection: Moses and Elijah both encountered God on Mount Sinai. These encounters were also revelations. On the mountain, Moses received the Ten Commandments and Elijah received a new and significant vocation (1 Kings 19:18). Peter, James, and John witnessed an eye-opening disclosure. Jesus is bathed in dazzling light and a voice from heaven declares Jesus is God's 'Son, the Beloved.' This event, known to us as 'the Transfiguration' is most often interpreted to have implications, not only for how we understand Jesus, but how as believers we should see the whole of God's creation. If God's shining presence can be seen in the face and clothing of Jesus, then perhaps the eyes of faith will see God's shining presence in everything: the sound of birdsong, a kind and unexpected act or a vulnerable child in need of care.

The entire Holy Land is scattered with low mountains and hilly ranges. Jerusalem is a hilly city which affords several spectacular vistas onto the ancient parts of the Holy City and also views into the wilderness. It is the geography of the land which Jesus and all the Biblical characters were familiar with as their physical environment. The land helped to shape their understanding of God and their experience of faith. Pilgrims to the Holy Land often find that travelling in and walking this land causes them to gain a fresh understanding of Jesus, the entire Biblical story and sometimes of their own experience of God.

I have a strong and important memory of being on pilgrimage on the island of Iona off the West coast of Scotland. One day, our church group of adults and children made the climb up Dun I, the highest point of the island. It was a typical island day in October—grey and blowing a gale. When we got to the top we were almost immediately blown right back down to the bottom. We had a memorable half an hour on top, buffeted by the weather and laughing together at the power of the wind. I was struck then and have remembered ever since that overwhelming sense of the force of nature which spoke to me of God's invigorating creative power. It was only really possible to have that experience at the

The Church of the Transfiguration, Mount Tabor

top of Dun I. It seemed to bring us all close to God in an unusual way.

COVID-19 has given many people a fresh appreciation of their local, natural environment. Walks intended first as a means of getting out of the house and exercising have led people to see things in nature that they have previously missed. Prayerful walking can also help us to perceive the presence of God in our locality or in our favourite walking places. In the Nicene Creed, we declare that 'through (Christ) all things were made,' in which case, we should anticipate that we receive intimations (or more) of Jesus Christ in the world, in its natural beauty, in the love and generosity of others, and in the faces of people in need in our world. Perhaps Jesus's disciples were open to the revelation of Christ's true identity because of the resplendent beauty of what they saw on and from Mount Tabor. We too can have heart and mind opened to fresh insights as we explore the beauty of creation.

2. *Watch the Film*

The film for Week 3, "The Mountain," can be accessed by typing https://youtu.be/IfrjW-T3As4 into your browser. Alternatively, use the QR code on your mobile or cell phone.

3. *Read the Scriptures*

This week, reflect on the Gospel of Matthew 17:1-13. Read the passage once or twice and spend some time considering the details of the story.

1 Six days later, Jesus took with him Peter and James and his brother John and led them up a high mountain, by themselves. **2** And he was transfigured before them, and his face shone like the sun, and his clothes became dazzling white. **3** Suddenly there appeared to them Moses and Elijah, talking with him. **4** Then Peter said to Jesus, "Lord, it is good for us to be here; if you wish, I will make three dwellings here, one for you, one for Moses, and one for Elijah." **5** While he was still speaking, suddenly a bright cloud overshadowed them, and from the cloud a voice said, "This is my Son, the Beloved; with him I am well pleased; listen to him!" **6** When the disciples heard this, they fell to the ground and were overcome by fear. **7** But Jesus came and touched them, saying, "Get up and do not be afraid." **8** And when they looked up, they saw no one except Jesus himself alone.

9 As they were coming down the mountain, Jesus ordered them, "Tell no one about the vision until after the Son of Man has been raised from the dead." **10** And the disciples asked him, "Why, then, do the scribes say that Elijah must come first?" **11** He replied, "Elijah is indeed coming and will restore all things; **12** but I tell you that Elijah has already come, and they did not recognize him, but they did to him whatever they pleased. So also, the Son of Man is about to suffer at their hands." **13** Then the disciples understood that he was speaking to them about John the Baptist.

4. *Ask Questions*

1. Is the story of the Transfiguration one that draws you in and speaks to you, or one that feels hard to penetrate? Explore your reactions and what appeals or does not appeal to you in the story.

2. What does the image of Jesus 'shining like the sun . . . his clothes white as the light' suggest to you? How does it affect how you see and understand Jesus?

3. Have you had a 'mountain top experience'? Share this or write it down to explore your experience; perhaps it might inspire a poem or a sketch.

4. How can you begin or continue to cherish nature as a place to experience God?

5. In the film there is a point made about 'seeing things differently' or seeing from the perspective of the 'divine eye.' What does this mean to you?

You might like to spend some time in prayer.

You might like to reflect further on this session and write down anything you want to hold on to.

WEEK FOUR
THE
SEA

The Sea of Galilee from the northern shore

1. *Reflection*

The Sea of Galilee has a special place in the faith and heart of every Christian. So many of us grew up with the stories of Jesus and all that he did on and around the Sea of Galilee. It feels like a familiar place to us even before we have actually visited it in person, so, when we do make our pilgrimage to the Holy Land, there can be a sense of feeling as if we have arrived in our spiritual home when we get to Galilee. The sea is a place of great beauty: a large expanse of (usually) blue water, circled by high hills on all sides which afford spectacular views across the sea's length and breadth.

Actually 'sea' is a misnomer because it contains freshwater, rather than saltwater, and it is considerably smaller than other seas. The origin for this anomaly lay in the fact that the Hebrew word for 'sea' (*yam*) can be used interchangeably with the word 'lake.' Nevertheless, like any other sea it is certainly subject to difficult weather conditions, so it is no surprise that the disciples could become terrified

The Sea from Kibbutz Ginnosar

in a storm while out on the sea in a boat. But the most usual experience for pilgrims and other visitors is of an attractive expanse of water, which, when either walking beside it or sailing on it, conveys a sense of peace and beauty.

When contemplating the Sea of Galilee, there are so many events in Jesus's ministry on which one could focus. The calling of the first disciples took place on the shoreline as the Lord saw Simon Peter and Andrew busy in their work, fishing (Mark 1:16-18). He invited them to leave their nets and follow him. There is the time when Jesus amazingly calmed the storm when the disciples feared for their lives. Jesus's ministry comes to a conclusion by the sea too (John 21:4-14). Following his resurrection, Christ

The Sea of Galilee from the Mount of Beatitudes

appears to the disciples as they are fishing on the sea and cooks them up a breakfast of bread and fish.

Several events in Jesus's ministry around the sea are commemorated by churches built on the shoreline, and these are favourite stopping points for pilgrims. But in my view, there is nothing better than finding a quiet spot to sit by oneself and meditate on the biblical stories and the call of Christ upon your own life.

Even if we do not all have the chance to spend time in this place of natural beauty and spiritual significance, many people will have favourite places to walk or to visit in which the presence of God readily becomes real. During the COVID-19 pandemic many people re-discovered the joy of walking and enjoying God's creation. Perhaps the sea, a lake, or a river

The Mediterranean Sea at Jaffa

can draw us into the presence of God in a special way. It was by the Sea of Galilee that Jesus called the disciples away from their occupation as fishermen to a vocation of living and proclaiming God's redeeming love. They were receptive to the voice of God in that moment.

However, the enrichment we can receive from time spent contemplating by the Sea of Galilee is rather a contrast to how people of Jesus's time felt and thought about the sea. Jews back then, and even today, would typically refer to themselves as 'people of the Land.' The Land was promised to Moses (Exod 6:6-8), and when eventually they crossed the Jordan, they took possession of the Land. They saw their occupation of Judea and Samaria as a sign of God's blessing. However, the sea, whether that be the large inland water expanses or the Mediterranean Sea, was viewed with suspicion and fear. The Philistines were the 'Sea People,' and the sea was associated with chaos, danger, and fearful sea monsters who lived in the deeps.

For this reason, the story of Jesus's calming of the storm has even more significance than we tend to understand in our own reading of the text.

"The disciples went and woke Jesus saying, 'Lord, we are perishing.' And he said to them, 'Why are you afraid, you of little faith?'" (Matt 8:23-27).

Meanwhile, Jesus had been peacefully sleeping in the back of the boat. Of course, we know exactly what Jesus did to save the day. We are not surprised that the disciples were frightened, and we can identify with their panic.

This is a reminder to us in all situations, not only if we are in a storm in a boat, but at all times, to trust in God who can help us to overcome paralysing fear and to do what needs to be done. In the midst of the coronavirus pandemic, the Bishop of London, Sarah Mullally, reflecting on the isolating and frightening experience of a lockdown confining so many to their homes, suggested that we all should focus on God rather than on the virus, to find some solace. For, in the story of the storm-calming, Jesus told the disciples to focus on him rather than on the storm. The disciples saw that Jesus had power over the elements, everything became peaceful again, and they were reassured. Jesus, the Saviour of the world, was

45

Sunrise over the Sea of Galilee

more powerful than the forces of the abyss of which they were so afraid.

Looking out across the gentle stillness of the Sea of Galilee we might just be able to sense the peace which can be ours through faith. Inevitably there will be times when we are fearful, and we cannot expect God simply to work magic to protect us from all dangers. But our faith in the goodness and the power of God can give to us a peace which passes all understanding. You may well have your own sense of danger lurking around the corner in the midst of your situation right now, just as people of Jesus' time believed there were fearful monsters inhabiting the depths of the abyss. Nearer to home, any one of us can find a place, on the shore of a lake or walking along a beach, and find that same sense

46

of equilibrium which comes from the confidence of faith in the God who is strong to save.

The beautiful nineteenth-century hymn written by Horatio Bonar wonderfully captures that hope which I glimpse every time I walk beside the Sea of Galilee.

> I heard the voice of Jesus say,
> "I am this dark world's light;
> Look unto me, your morn shall rise,
> And all your days be bright."
> I looked to Jesus, and I found
> In him my star, my sun;
> And in that light of life I'll walk
> Till trav'ling days are done.

2. Watch the Film

The film for Week 4, "The Sea," can be accessed by typing https://youtu.be/mgTU1dburBI into your browser. Alternatively, use the QR code on your mobile or cell phone.

3. Read the Scriptures

This week, reflect on the Gospel of Matthew 8:23-27.

Read the passage once or twice and spend some time considering the details of the story.

23 And when Jesus got into the boat, his disciples followed him. 24 A windstorm arose on the sea, so great that the boat was being swamped by the waves; but he was asleep. 25 And they went and woke him up, saying, "Lord, save us! We are perishing!" 26 And he said to them, "Why are you afraid, you of little faith?" Then he got up and rebuked the winds and the sea; and there was a dead calm. 27 They were amazed, saying, "What sort of man is this, that even the winds and the sea obey him?"

4. *Ask Questions*

1. Spend time recalling when you have been beside the Sea of Galilee or another body of water that is special to you. What do you recall of your experience of God in that place? Does this memory speak into your present situation or experience? What grace is offered to you today through this process of memory?

2. In the Gospels, fear is such a common reaction of the disciples. Do you connect with their reactions of fear? Reflect on your own reactions of fear. What do you notice in your body? Are there any patterns in your responses? What is God like in the place of your fear? What does God say to you through these and other gospel stories?

3. The gospel accounts of Jesus's calming of the storm encourage us to look at Jesus rather than the source of our fear or our distress. Can you recall a time when you have done this? Share this experience with others (if you can) and what you discovered about yourself and God.

4. What hymns or pieces of music help to calm you when you are unsettled or worried?

You might like to spend some time in prayer.

You might like to reflect further on this session and write down anything you want to hold on to.

WEEK FIVE

THE
ROAD

Overview of the Old City of Jerusalem

1. *Reflection*

This fifth week of the Lent study sets us on course for Jerusalem. The road to Jerusalem was well-trodden by the Jews of Palestine in Jesus's time and before, because pilgrimage to the Holy City and to the Temple for the great festivals was a requirement. A crux moment in Jesus's life in Luke's Gospel is when Jesus 'set his face to go to Jerusalem' (Luke 9:51) and culminates in his Triumphal Entry on what has become known to the Church as Palm Sunday.

Much has been written about the journey motif in scripture—it is a continuing theme throughout. Journey is so foundational to the Christian story of salvation that it has also become a way of understanding our entire Christian life; it is a journey from start to finish. Indeed, the concept of pilgrimage is itself a development of the idea that a journey lies at the heart of Christian experience. For a pilgrim, the final destination is deeply significant but the journey along the way is almost as important. Lent itself,

The Judean Desert

from Ash Wednesday to Easter, is a journey, and on this virtual Lenten pilgrimage we have come a long way via the desert, a watering hole, a mountain, and the sea. Now we can look backwards and also forwards on this road we are travelling with Jesus.

The road and the concept of a journey is a theme which reaches back into the Old Testament; it provides a template for Jesus in his ministry and also perhaps for us as Christian pilgrims. Abraham sets out from Ur and then Haran to find the land promised to him by God (Gen 11-13). Moses led the people out of slavery and through the desert. Eventually, under Joshua's leadership, the people journeyed into the Promised Land (Josh 1-3). Perhaps most significantly, God opens up a road for the Jews to return from exile in Babylon to repopulate

Jerusalem and Judea in the 6th century BC (Ezra 1). This return was described so powerfully by the prophet Isaiah when he said: 'A voice cries out in the wilderness, prepare the way of the Lord, make straight in the desert a highway for our God' (Isa 40:3).

All of these texts and events in the Old Testament serve as part of the backdrop for Jesus's own ministry. As mentioned previously when considering the desert, the gospel writers, and especially Matthew, conceive of Jesus as a new Moses, not leading people physically from one place to another but leading them, and us, spiritually from a place of bondage (sin) to a place of freedom (salvation). When Christians come to the Holy Land on pilgrimage they want, perhaps more than anything else, to walk in the footsteps of Jesus on the road he took for us, to effect our salvation.

Each one of us will have our own sense of the journey of our life with its high peaks and, in Bunyan's evocative phrase, our 'slough(s) of despond.' For us, as for Bunyan's Pilgrim, we are drawn ever onwards to the 'Celestial City.' Perhaps many people using this study course will have experienced a pilgrimage, either to the Holy Land, or other pilgrim destinations whether near, or far from home. If so, then there is ample material for prayerful contemplation of a purposeful journey with a spiritual goal. One of my most enriching experiences of pilgrimage was along the ancient Pilgrims' Way from Winchester to Canterbury in England. That journey of 135

A road through the desert from Jerusalem to Jericho

miles, lasting some two weeks, travelling with twelve others, taught me a great deal about the value of walking, praying, and talking together on pilgrimage. The common goal of ending in Canterbury was important but, actually, no less so than the daily goal of not losing our way and finding a meal and a bed at the end of each day. We found God's grace in the practical challenges as well as in the praying and story-sharing along the way.

Jesus's own journey recounted in the second half of Luke's Gospel, has been described by many commentators as 'The Road to Jerusalem.' It starts with Jesus setting his face in the direction of the Holy City and then in the ensuing ten chapters (Luke 9-19), Jesus makes a geographically circuitous, but a

*The Mount of Olives—Dominus Flevit Church
can be seen top right*

theological straight line, to his confrontation with the powers and authorities of his time.

In his commentary on Luke's Gospel, Fred Craddock suggests that the reader is 'drawn by Luke's presentation of Jesus's journey to Jerusalem into a pilgrimage with Jesus in an unfolding and deepening way, not only to the Passion but into the kingdom of God.'[1] For Jesus, this journey to Jerusalem reaches its peak on the donkey-riding, palm-strewn, hallelujah-singing procession into the city which 'kills the prophets and stones those who are sent to it' (Luke 13:34). Jesus is feted by the crowds as his journey to Jerusalem seemingly comes to a triumphal climax as he walks from Bethphage.

---

[1] Fred B. Jr. Craddock, *Luke*, Interpretation (Louisville, Kentucky: John Knox Press, 1990).

For many pilgrims to the Holy Land, the walk down the Mount of Olives, stopping at the Church of Dominus Flevit to remember Jesus's tears over the city, and then up the other side of the Kidron Valley into the Old City, is a powerful devotional journey. This might then dovetail into walking the Stations of the Cross along the Via Dolorosa, finally to arrive at the Church of the Holy Sepulchre in order to pray at the Golgotha Chapel and then at the tomb of burial and resurrection.

In normal times, as opposed to these pandemic years, many churches would re-enact the procession into Jerusalem in their own neighbourhood on Palm Sunday. In doing so, Christians seek to re-capture that atmosphere of the praise before the betrayal and the passion as a way to enter into the rigours of Holy Week.

In a sense, a Lenten study, as with a pilgrimage, seeks to enable people to enter into the events of Jesus's life to help them better to understand the nature of God's gift to them and their calling as disciples following Jesus's way. A pilgrimage to the Land of the Holy One can help us to enter into Jesus's own journey because we can sense for ourselves the heat of the day, the steepness of the road, the vistas from the mountaintop, and the calm of the waters. But wherever we are and wherever we go, the essence of the Christian life is to gain a heightened awareness of where God desires us to be and what God calls us to do. These are the questions at the heart of our life-long pilgrimage journey, the road of

Ninth Station on the Via Dolorosa

faith on which we travel. The Celtic blessing puts it beautifully: May the road rise up to meet you, may the wind be always at you back; soft rains fall upon your fields, and until we meet again, may God be with you.

2. *Watch the Film*

The film for Week 5, "The Road," can be accessed by typing https://youtu.be/hrV7kxjPJMg into your browser. Alternatively, use the QR code on your mobile or cell phone.

3. *Read the Scriptures*

This week, reflect on the Gospel of Luke 19:28-47. Read the passage once or twice and spend some time considering the details of the story.

28 After he had said this, he went on ahead, going up to Jerusalem.

29 When he had come near Bethphage and Bethany, at the place called the Mount of Olives, he sent two of the disciples, 30 saying, "Go into the village ahead of you, and as you enter it you will find tied there a colt that has never been ridden. Untie it and bring it here. 31 If anyone asks you, 'Why are you untying it?' just say this, 'The Lord needs it.'" 32 So those who were sent departed and found it as he had told them. 33 As they were untying the colt, its owners asked them, "Why are you untying the colt?" 34 They said, "The Lord needs it." 35 Then they brought it to Jesus; and after throwing their cloaks on the colt, they set Jesus on it. 36 As he rode along,

people kept spreading their cloaks on the road. ³⁷ As he was now approaching the path down from the Mount of Olives, the whole multitude of the disciples began to praise God joyfully with a loud voice for all the deeds of power that they had seen, ³⁸ saying,

> "Blessed is the king
>   who comes in the name of the Lord!
> Peace in heaven,
>   and glory in the highest heaven!"

³⁹ Some of the Pharisees in the crowd said to him, "Teacher, order your disciples to stop." ⁴⁰ He answered, "I tell you, if these were silent, the stones would shout out."

⁴¹ As he came near and saw the city, he wept over it, ⁴² saying, "If you, even you, had only recognized on this day the things that make for peace! But now they are hidden from your eyes. ⁴³ Indeed, the days will come upon you, when your enemies will set up ramparts around you and surround you, and hem you in on every side. ⁴⁴ They will crush you to the ground, you and your children within you, and they will not leave within you one stone upon another; because you did not recognize the time of your visitation from God."

⁴⁵ Then he entered the temple and began to drive out those who were selling things there; ⁴⁶ and he said, "It is written,

> 'My house shall be a house of prayer';
>   but you have made it a den of robbers."

[47] Every day he was teaching in the temple. The chief priests, the scribes, and the leaders of the people kept looking for a way to kill him.

4. *Ask Questions*

1. Thinking back on your life, consider some moments when the journey was hard. What was it that sustained you? In the 'sunny uplands,' describe how you felt. You might like to write a short account of either, or a poem?

2. Jesus 'set his face towards Jerusalem;' do you think that you have set your face towards someone, something, or somewhere? How does this affect your life and your priorities?

3. As Jesus walked down the Mount of Olives and saw Jerusalem, he wept over it. What do you think Jesus weeps over in our world today, in your city or neighbourhood? What difference does that make to us?

4. Palm Sunday captures a mood of joy although it stands at the start of Holy Week, with the difficult days which follow. What gives you joy in the midst of the challenges of your life's journey past and present? How can we nurture that joy? You might like to write down some ideas that you can commit to for the weeks ahead to help you face life's challenges.

You might like to spend some time in prayer.

You might like to reflect further on this session and write down anything you want to hold on to.

WEEK SIX

THE
GARDEN

Natural beauty near the source of the River Jordan

1. *Reflection*

It has often been noted that the Bible begins in a garden with a tree whose fruit leads to the first sin (Gen 2 and 3) and ends with the New Jerusalem in which there is a tree whose 'leaves are for the healing of the nations' (Rev 22:1-5). John Milton described this powerfully in the 17th century in his epic poems *Paradise Lost* and *Paradise Regained.* It might not be entirely incidental that Jesus sought his Father's will also in a garden (Gethsemane) and sought the strength to fulfil his divine calling, which of course he did (Matt 26:36-56).

Adam and Eve's failure to obey God's will in the Garden of Eden is mirrored in opposite by Jesus's faithful following of God's will in Gethsemane.

One who has not visited the Holy Land might suffer the misapprehension that gardens and green landscapes do not feature significantly there. But the region between the Mediterranean and the River Jordan has a surprising variety of vegetation and flora. In the north around the Galilee region,

The gardens of the Scots Hotel, Tiberias

plentiful rainfall and a tropical climate create conditions for lush countryside especially in winter and spring (see picture above). In the south of the country, from Jerusalem westwards towards the Mediterranean, there are excellent conditions for fruit trees and good arable land. There are good reasons why the Promised Land is described as a 'land flowing with milk and honey' (Exod 3:8); in other words, it is rich and fertile. Even in the desert there are beautiful oases. Especially noteworthy is Jericho, which even today is a source of the most wonderful fruit—dates, bananas, oranges and much more.

For so many people living in urbanized centres, a garden is a little piece of personal paradise. Especially in a time of pandemic-induced lockdown, our gardens became a refuge for sanity and wellbeing. Time spent planting and nurturing, pruning and clearing can be so helpful for our mental and spiritual health. Or perhaps, without a garden, many have found that a walk in the woods or in a local park has become vital, whilst aspects of normal life to which we were accustomed have been missing. We are also aware that the entire planet we inhabit is akin to a garden. To damage its delicate balance is to threaten the existence of creation itself.

So, whilst the mythical story of Adam and Eve in the Garden of Eden does not give us an historical account of the beginnings of human life on earth, it does convey deep and significant truths about the human condition and our need for healing and salvation. It's a description of human nature and our relationship with the rest of creation which resonates throughout the biblical narrative in the Old and New Testaments. For instance, St. Paul writes in 1 Corinthians: 'For since death came through a human being, the resurrection has also come through a human being; for as all die in Adam, so all will be made alive in Christ' (1 Cor 15:21-22).

After Jesus's Last Supper with his disciples in an 'Upper Room' in Jerusalem, he then takes his friends out of the city to the garden of Gethsemane. Perhaps it was a convenient place away from crowds and a good place to pray under the stars. It may not have been accidental that an act of betrayal was fixed to take place in a garden amongst the olive trees—a betrayal that would lead to reconciliation

The Garden of Gethsemane under a full moon

between God and humanity, for it was the rebellion of Adam and Eve which (at least mythically speaking) accounts for the breach between God and humanity.

It is a great blessing that the garden of Gethsemane still exists in Jerusalem and is a major focus of Christian devotion for all those who make their Holy Land pilgrimage. It is a place Christians can come to contemplate the courage and sacrifice of Christ as he pleaded, 'Let this cup pass from me' (Matt 26:39). Everyone who stops here can consider the conflicts and weighty decisions which trouble them, even if they do not compare to the significance of the moment when Jesus prayed there and sweated droplets of blood.

When I have had big decisions to make, I have often taken myself to the sacred space of a church, but I am also often drawn to a place in nature, perhaps a secluded garden, from where I can gain a sense of perspective away from the noise of

Wrought iron door of olive trees

contemporary life and its multiple device distractions. Personally, I am not given to expect direct divine guidance, but time for the calming of the inner chatter in a pastoral-type context often seems to bring more clarity.

The Church of All Nations in Gethsemane, designed and built by the brilliant architect Antonio

The Church of Nations on the Mount of Olives

Barluzzi, manages to combine both church and garden in his design; it is also called the Church of the Agony. The doors into the church are made of wrought iron. The ancient, twisted tree design gives the effect of walking into an olive grove. The interior of the church is stubbornly dark, evoking night time as if every time one walks into this church, one is transported to that first fateful Maundy Thursday evening. Christians take great comfort from the account of Jesus's agonized prayers and ultimate submission to the will of God. The unfolding of events is instructive for us: as with Jesus, our prayers should avoid trying (as if we could) to change God's mind or telling God what to do. It is more appropriate that we should seek to have our minds and ways changed by the will of God. To discern God's will for us is the great challenge of faith.

As Lent comes to the climax of Holy Week, we are drawn deeper into that drama of Jesus's willing but costly sacrifice. Stopping for a moment in the Garden of Gethsemane to pray as if we were with

A pathway in the Garden of Gethsemane

Jesus in his hour of testing, can help us to contemplate our own lives and the needs of the world. We are indeed a long way from the garden of Eden and its imagery of harmonious co-existence within the created order. In one post-resurrection encounter, Jesus is mistaken for a gardener, which might suggest to us, as we contemplate the current state of the world, that our faith might enable us to recover something of that harmony. But the climate crisis tells us that we have an urgent and challenging task to address. We have exploited the garden which God has created, even though God called us to be its stewards.

Our Lenten journey comes to a conclusion here in this moment of challenge as Jesus's journey reaches its decisive moment with a betrayal in the garden. But we know that the journey does not end there. In Jerusalem, spiritually, all roads lead to the Church of the Holy Sepulchre, that shrine which for nearly two thousand years has been venerated as the place of crucifixion and the place of resurrection. Whatever the challenges or difficulties in Lent, or during our lives in general, as Christians we know that the decisive reality above everything else is the resurrection. It is that event and its message of victory of light over dark and life over death which can sustain us in our continuing Christian pilgrimage.

2. *Watch the Film*

The film for Week 6, "The Garden," can be accessed by typing https://youtu.be/459aM2ApC8E into your browser. Alternatively, use the QR code on your mobile or cell phone.

3. *Read the Scriptures*

This week, reflect on the Gospel of Matthew 26:36-56. Read the passage once or twice and spend some time considering the details of the story.

36 Then Jesus went with them to a place called Gethsemane; and he said to his disciples, "Sit here while

I go over there and pray." [37] He took with him Peter and the two sons of Zebedee, and began to be grieved and agitated. [38] Then he said to them, "I am deeply grieved, even to death; remain here, and stay awake with me." [39] And going a little farther, he threw himself on the ground and prayed, "My Father, if it is possible, let this cup pass from me; yet not what I want but what you want." [40] Then he came to the disciples and found them sleeping; and he said to Peter, "So, could you not stay awake with me one hour? [41] Stay awake and pray that you may not come into the time of trial; the spirit indeed is willing, but the flesh is weak." [42] Again he went away for the second time and prayed, "My Father, if this cannot pass unless I drink it, your will be done." [43] Again he came and found them sleeping, for their eyes were heavy. [44] So leaving them again, he went away and prayed for the third time, saying the same words. [45] Then he came to the disciples and said to them, "Are you still sleeping and taking your rest? See, the hour is at hand, and the Son of Man is betrayed into the hands of sinners. [46] Get up, let us be going. See, my betrayer is at hand."

[47] While he was still speaking, Judas, one of the twelve, arrived; with him was a large crowd with swords and clubs, from the chief priests and the elders of the people. [48] Now the betrayer had given them a sign, saying, "The one I will kiss is the man; arrest him." [49] At once he came up to Jesus and said, "Greetings, Rabbi!" and kissed him. [50] Jesus said to him, "Friend, do what you are here to do." Then they

came and laid hands on Jesus and arrested him. ⁵¹ Suddenly, one of those with Jesus put his hand on his sword, drew it, and struck the slave of the high priest, cutting off his ear. ⁵² Then Jesus said to him, "Put your sword back into its place; for all who take the sword will perish by the sword. ⁵³ Do you think that I cannot appeal to my Father, and he will at once send me more than twelve legions of angels? ⁵⁴ But how then would the scriptures be fulfilled, which say it must happen in this way?" ⁵⁵ At that hour Jesus said to the crowds, "Have you come out with swords and clubs to arrest me as though I were a bandit? Day after day I sat in the temple teaching, and you did not arrest me. ⁵⁶ But all this has taken place, so that the scriptures of the prophets may be fulfilled." Then all the disciples deserted him and fled.

4. *Ask Questions*

1. Imagine yourself in that garden with the other disciples accompanying Jesus as he prays. As Jesus moves away from you to pray alone, what do you feel and think? Do you speak to the other disciples? If so, what do you say—what do they say in response? Do you stay with them? If so, what happens?

2. Although Jesus says to stay and wait, do you follow after him? What do you see and hear? How do you want to respond to Jesus? Pray through,

or share with others, what this imaginative exercise revealed.

3. Why is it hard to stay focused in prayer? What helps you to use your time of prayer fruitfully?

4. In the introduction to *Paradise Lost*, Milton prays for assistance in his creative task asking God: 'What is dark within me, illumine.' This is a courageous request. Often, we prefer not to see our dark places. In what ways and to what effect can God illumine the dark places in you, in the world?

5. In the 1970s, in the song "Woodstock," Crosby, Stills and Nash sang:

> 'We are stardust, we are golden,
> we are billion year old carbon,
> And we've got to get back to the garden.'

For you, what could it mean to 'get back to the garden?' You might like to represent this in a sketch or painting, a clay sculpture, a poem or a song or piece of music without words.

6. As Lent draws to a close, what are the parts of this Lent course that you want to take with you into Holy Week and beyond?

You might like to spend some time in prayer.

You might like to reflect further on this session and write down anything you want to hold on to.

AFTERWORD

This study has led the reader on a journey through the Holy Land, noticing the features of the landscape and their essential part in the unfolding events of salvation. May all those who make this pilgrimage of the heart be encouraged and strengthened in their daily lives. For those able to make a pilgrimage to the Holy Land, there is nothing like seeing these places in reality. For anyone who can return for another pilgrimage, there is almost certainly more to discover. St George's College, Jerusalem runs study pilgrimages throughout the year. All of these can be seen and bookings can be made via the College website.

St. George's College
P.O. Box 1248
33 Salah El Deen Street
Jerusalem 91000
www.saintgeorgescollegejerusalem.com

The Very Rev. Canon Richard Sewell is the Dean of St. George's College, Jerusalem. He is British and has previously served as a priest in the Diocese of Southwark in the UK. His last post before moving to Jerusalem was as Team Rector of Barnes Team Ministry, which comprises three churches in South West London. Richard was ordained priest on the Feast of St. Francis, 2003. He trained for ministry at SEITE, now St. Augustine's College. He also studied Theology at the University of Birmingham for his B.A. He did further studies at Heythrop College for an M.A. in Biblical Studies.

His first encounter with the Holy Land was working as a volunteer for the Church of Scotland

Hospice (now The Scots Hotel) in Tiberias in the 1980s. For three years he ran an Inter-Faith Project in East London.

Prior to ordination Richard worked for the Anglican Mission Agency, USPG, as a mission educator with additional responsibilities for USPG's relationship with the Churches in Pakistan and Bangladesh.

JulieAnn, his wife, trained as a Primary School Teacher, then Counsellor but in Jerusalem she volunteers in the Princess Basma Centre which works with children with disabilities. Their adult children, Nathaniel and Eliana, continue to pursue their careers and studies in the UK.

Richard, in addition to his role as Dean of the College, is a Residentiary Canon of St George's Cathedral, Jerusalem and is Honorary Canon of Southwark Cathedral in his home diocese in the Church of England. The Diocese of Southwark is Richard's sponsoring agency in his role as Dean. He loves Indie music, running for fitness, and walking in wildernesses.

Printed in Great Britain
by Amazon

17387620R00058